the Anti-Colouring book

To Michael J. Striker
Stephen, Howard and Rachel Kimmel

*Special thanks for their help and inspiration to Herbeta W. Stinkus,
Herb Perr, John Striker, Joan Imbrogno, and to all our students,
especially John Menge, Philip Popielarski, and Peter Popielarksi.*

*Grateful acknowledgement is made to Michele Irvin for permission
to reproduce her photograph.*

Scholastic Children's Books,
Commonwealth House, 1–19 New Oxford Street,
London WC1A 1NU, UK

A division of Scholastic Ltd
London ~ New York ~ Toronto ~ Sydney ~ Auckland
Mexico City ~ New Delhi ~ Hong Kong

First published in the USA by Holt, Rhinehart and Winston, 1978

First published in the UK by Scholastic Ltd, 1979
This edition published 2004

Copyright © Susan Striker and Edward Kimmel, 1978

ISBN 0 439 96328 1

Printed and bound in Finland by WS Bookwell

2 4 6 8 10 9 7 5 3 1

the Anti-Colouring book

Susan Striker
& Edward Kimmel

SCHOLASTIC

"If we pretend to respect the artist at all, we must allow ... freedom of choice ... Art derives a considerable part of its beneficial exercise from flying in the face of presumptions."

Henry James

You are a space pioneer. Design a flag for your new planet.

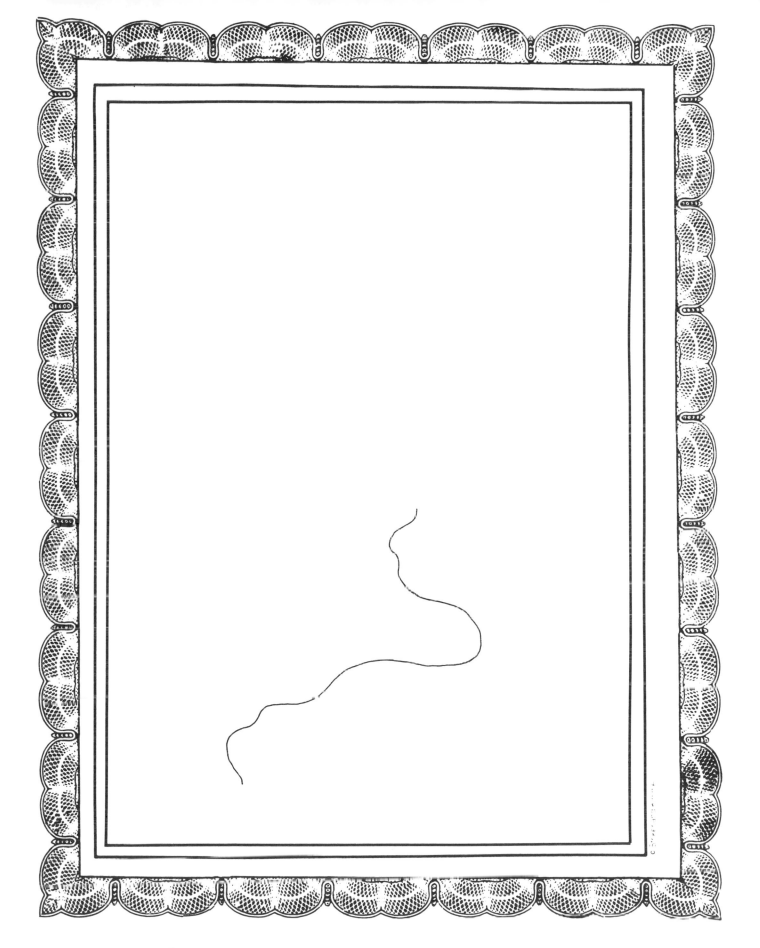

A famous artist needs your help. The artist started
this picture but was stung on the thumb by a bee.
Turn the picture any way you'd like and finish it.

Design a postage stamp for the first
letter mailed from Mars.

Name of fish: _Channelle_
Discovered by: _____
Place discovered: _____

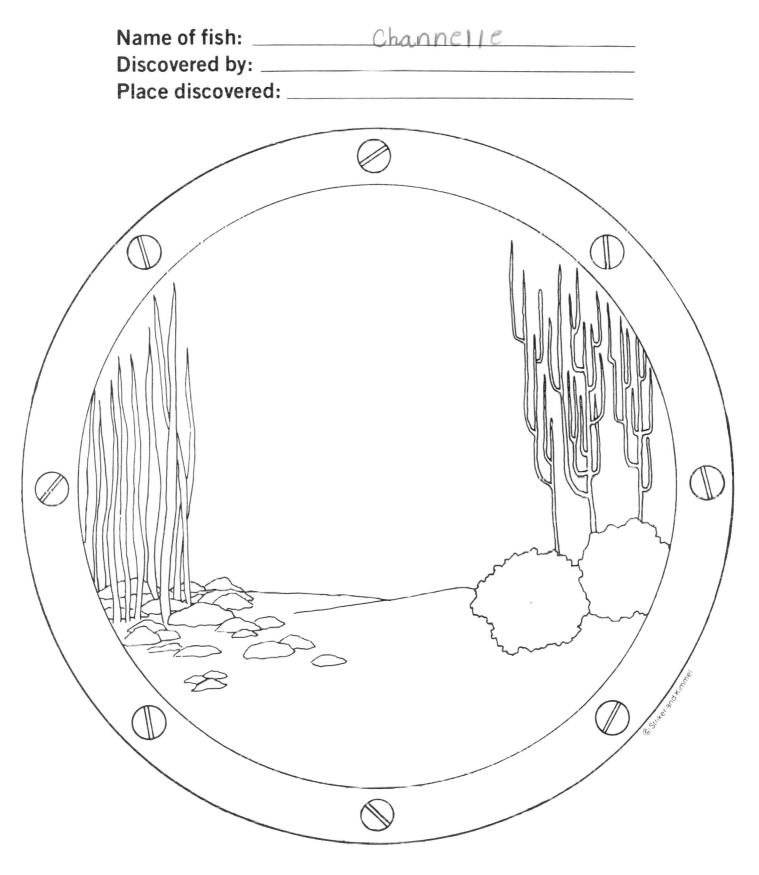

Scientists have just found a new species of fish, but they haven't named it yet. What do you think it looks like and what would you call it?

What was the nicest dream you ever had?

25¢ DAILY

Vol. 1 No. 1   I by oho II I : to ucynollo du cyal n s olu cldy oho II   © Striker and Kimmel

EXTRA! EXTRA!
MARTIANS LAND

FUNCTION: _____

DESIGN A ROBOT
THAT WILL DO A CHORE
YOU DON'T LIKE DOING

What would you do with a fortune?

You are a scuba diver and you have just made the most exciting underwater discovery. What have you found?

What is the photographer taking a picture of?

This clown has learned how to become invisible. We can
see only this circle. What part of the clown do you think the circle is?

Can you change this pair of scissors into
something completely different? Turn the
paper any way you want to.

*Design a family crest that tells something about you
and your family.*

©Striker and Kimmel

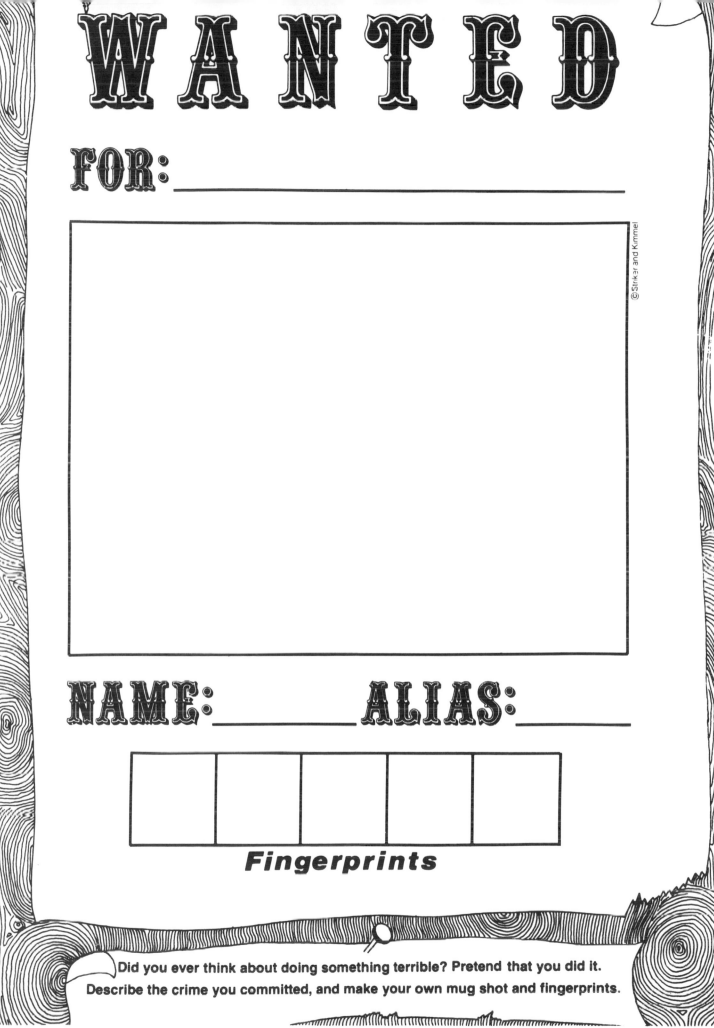

WANTED

FOR: _____

NAME: _____ ALIAS: _____

Fingerprints

Did you ever think about doing something terrible? Pretend that you did it.
Describe the crime you committed, and make your own mug shot and fingerprints.

©Striker and Kimmel

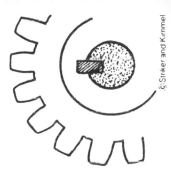

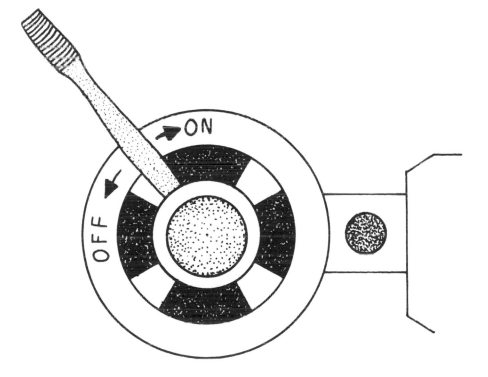

You have just invented a machine that will change the lives of everyone on earth. Only you understand the invention well enough to complete the picture.

What would you add to each scene to show the changes in the four seasons?

Do you see your future in this crystal ball?

© Striker and Kimmel

Today is your birthday. Inside this box is the
present you want most in the world. Can you see it?

FLOWER SOCIETY

Name of flower: _____

_____

Discovered by: _____

_____

Place discovered: _____

_____

What does it smell like? _____

_____

How do you know that it is poisonous? _____

_____

Size of blossom: _____

_____

Any other information: _____

_____

_____

_____

_____

_____

_____

_____

_____

_____

_____

You have discovered a poisonous flower growing in your garden. Scientists have asked you to draw a picture of it, name it, and tell something about how you found it.

What are these people looking at?

Where in the world would you like to go to see
a rainbow?

A group of
explorers found a rare bird
deep in the jungle. They sent
back this drawing of the bird
sitting in a tree.

Do you ever lie on your back and imagine that you see pictures
in the clouds? What do you see in these clouds?

The Daily Paper

20¢   *Vol. 12 No. 24*   **August 25, 1987**

HERO!

c Striker and Kimmel

You have just performed a heroic deed.
This is the picture and story in the newspaper the next day.

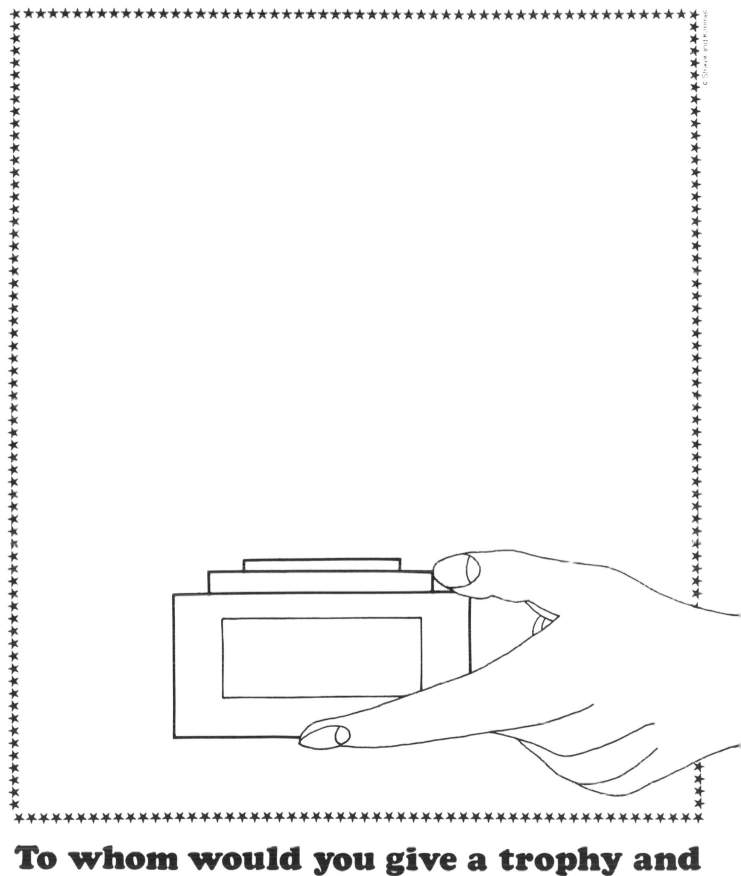

To whom would you give a trophy and what would it look like?

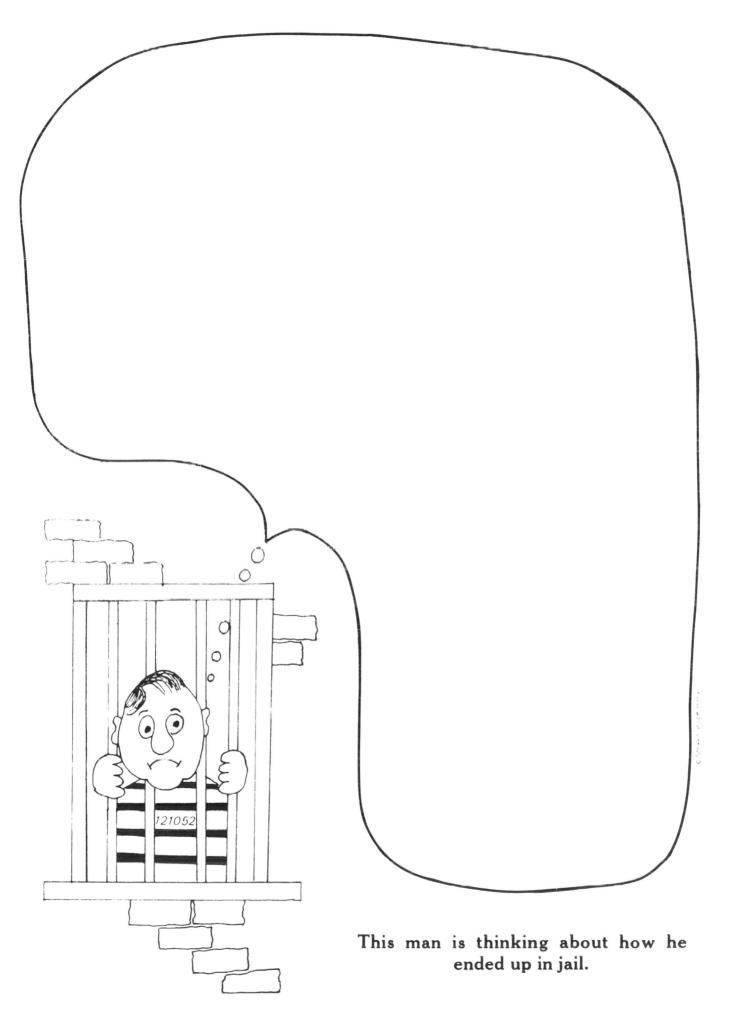

This man is thinking about how he
ended up in jail.

Half of this photograph is missing. Can you complete it?

Some people think there is a man or a woman in the moon, and others say the moon is made of green cheese. What do you think of when you look at the moon?

GOD

WHAT DO YOU THINK
GOD LOOKS LIKE?

_____

_____ ,

_____

_____

_____

_____

_____

_____

_____

_____

_____

_____

_____

_____ ,

_____

Write a letter to the person you like (or hate) most in the world.
Use pictures instead of words wherever possible.

These people can't decide which hats to buy. Can you help them make up their minds?

Space explorers have discovered flowers growing on the moons of Jupiter. What do they look like?

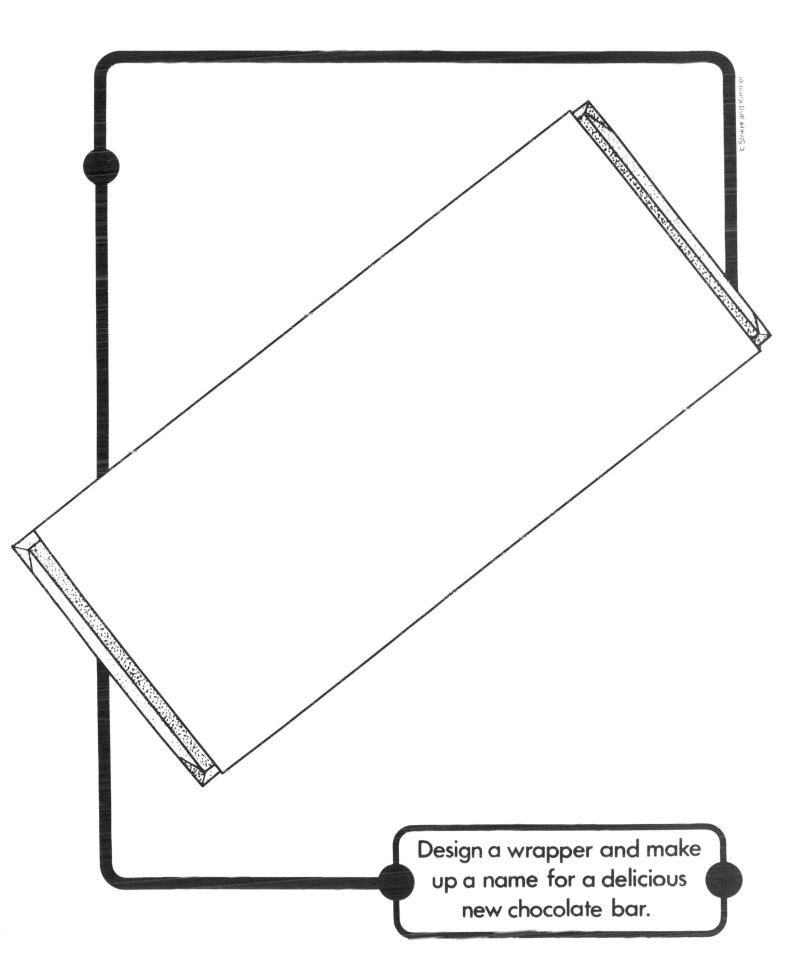

Design a wrapper and make up a name for a delicious new chocolate bar.

What kinds of transportation
will we have in the year 2010?

What do people do with their faces to show
how they are feeling?

This artist is about to paint a very strange picture. What will it look like?

STAR LIGHT, STAR BRIGHT
FIRST STAR I SEE TONIGHT

To Have

a nuwe Game a

fuss

What do you wish for?

© Striker and Kimmel

I WISH I MAY
I WISH I MIGHT
HAVE THE WISH
I WISH TONIGHT

Where are these birds flying to?

How do you look when you first get up in the morning?

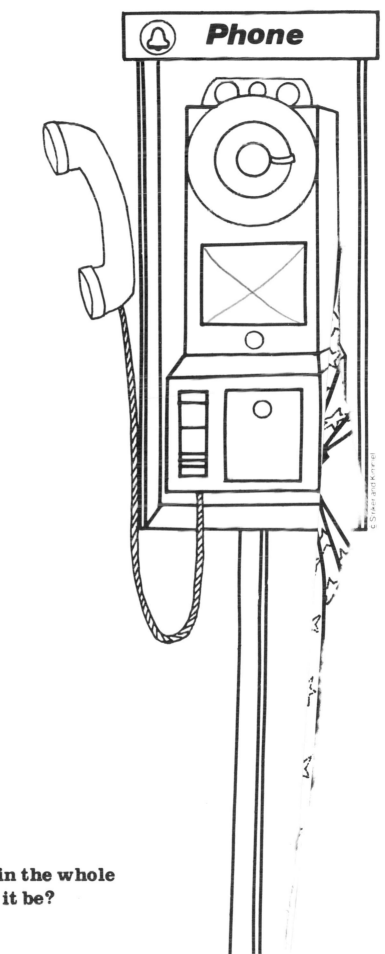

**If you could call anyone in the whole
world, who would it be?**

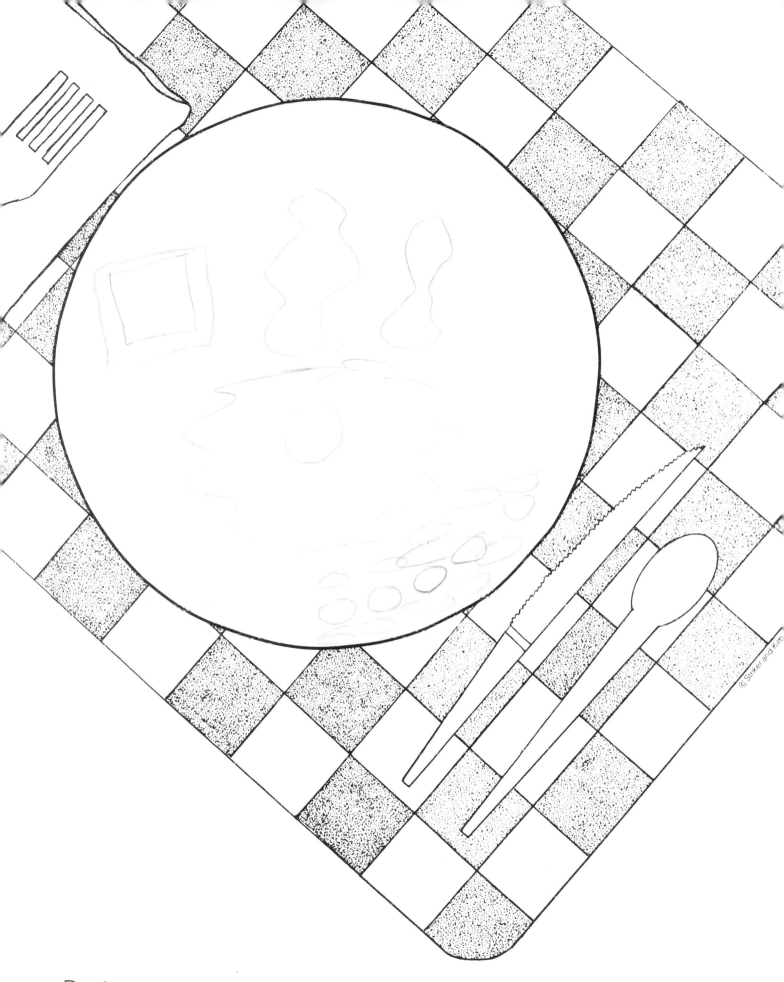

Design your own special dinner plate, to be used by you alone.

Oops! We spilled ink on the last page of this book. Can you turn it into a picture?